Windows 10:

Beginner's Guide on How to Get the Most out of Windows 10

Alexa Mitchell

CONTENTS

Thank you very much for getting this book!

I hope that you will really enjoy reading it. If you want to help me to produce more materials like this, then please leave a positive review on Amazon.

It really does make a difference!

Introduction

For many of us, Windows 10 is just a mere system that all of us feel like we were forced to deal with a while ago. It's been a few years since it came out, and it's been perfected, UT often, people either don't know how to use this, and it actually might not even be completely utilized. Think about it, do you truly know Windows 10?

Even those that have a decent knowledge of computers might not really know how to utilize Windows 10 to the best of their abilities, and that's where this book comes in. In this book, you'll learn how to completely immerse yourself into this, and you'll be able to use Windows 10 to your advantage, and be able to help update and maintain the system.

It's one of the best out there, and you can even customize it to the point where the annoying parts of this that you don't like are removed, such as the lock screen and other such factors. That's right; you can even remove some of the troublesome parts.

This book will go through everything that you need to know about this, from Cortana, to setting it up and disabling a few features hat you might not need, such as the constant updates and the security compromises, to even ways to enhance the experience, including how to get various files off from other parts of this, and how to rectify various bugs that might be there. With this book, you'll be able to become the true master of Windows 10 that you know that you want to be.

Lots of people tend to take this for granted. Oftentimes, they don't even realize just how important it to know your own computer. This book will give you everything that you need to know about this system, in order to have the best and most effective user experience that you can have with this.

Chapter 1 – Windows 10 Basics

The first thing to learn, are the basics of Windows 10. These are quite simple, and for someone that doesn't know anything about Windows 10, this is where you want to begin, because you'll be able to have a good footing for when you start to use this. Oftentimes even the basics aren't totally known by everyone, and often, we might leave some of the updates that you don't need to have on there, including the setting of locations and such. Be wary of this, start to work with this, and make the changes that are necessary in order to protect yourself and your computer as well.

Settings you want to change immediately

Now, before you begin, you will want to stop a few settings. These are put there in at the onset, and they're quite annoying. Here are a few things you can do to make the experience better.

First, you'll want to stop automatic updates. This is something that was initially released, and Microsoft didn't allow you to skip this. However, now you can, but if you're already in an update, you'll want to stop this. Automatic restart for updating is quite annoying, and unless you have it set to a schedule, you're going to be annoyed with this.

To fix this, go to the start menu, then click on advanced update, and then go to advanced Windows update options. Then, change the settings to "notify to schedule restart.

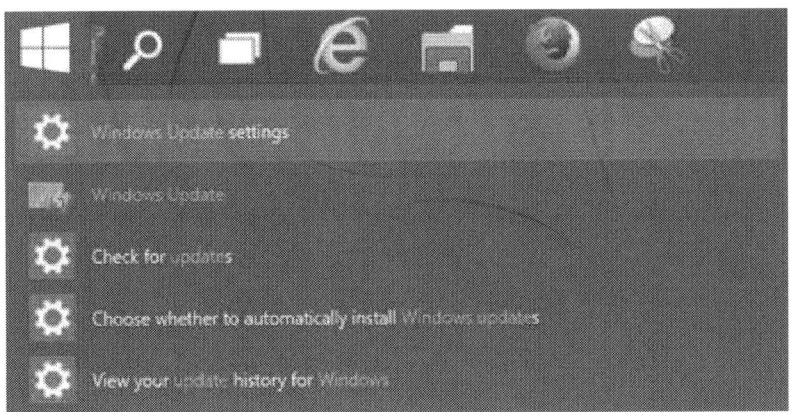

Keylogger is another one that you might want to disable because of the potential security problems with this. If you're worried, since it'll observe what you're typing, do the following: go to Start<settings<privacy settings<general option. Then, you can press the disable option on "Send Microsoft info about how I write to help use

improve typing and writing in the future." You can then look for another one that you'll want to find called "speech, inking, and typing" menu and then choose the option that reads "stop getting to know me." Make sure this is set to off.

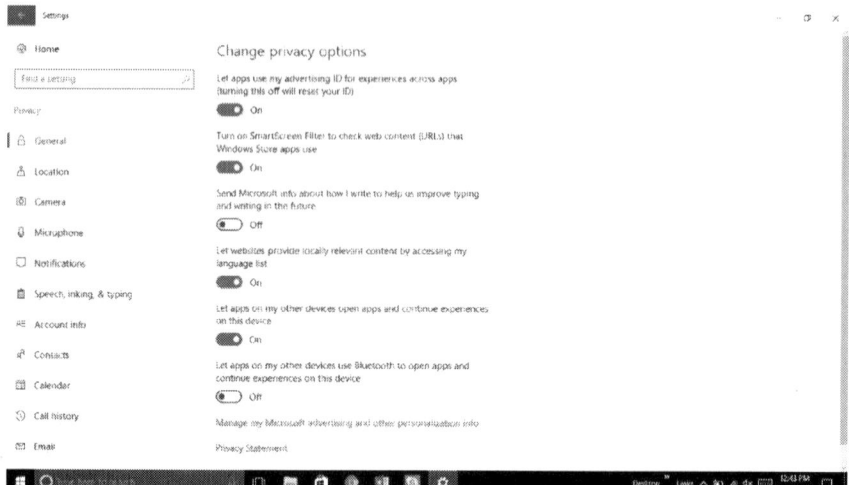

Finally, there are the notifications. This is annoying, and it creates pop-ups that look unseemly. How do you disable this then? Well, you go to settings>system>notifications and actions. From there, you can turn these off based on what you want to not see, such as the tips about Windows, any notifications, any sorts of lock screen notifications, and the like. It'll help reduce the clutter of your screen, making it look way better.

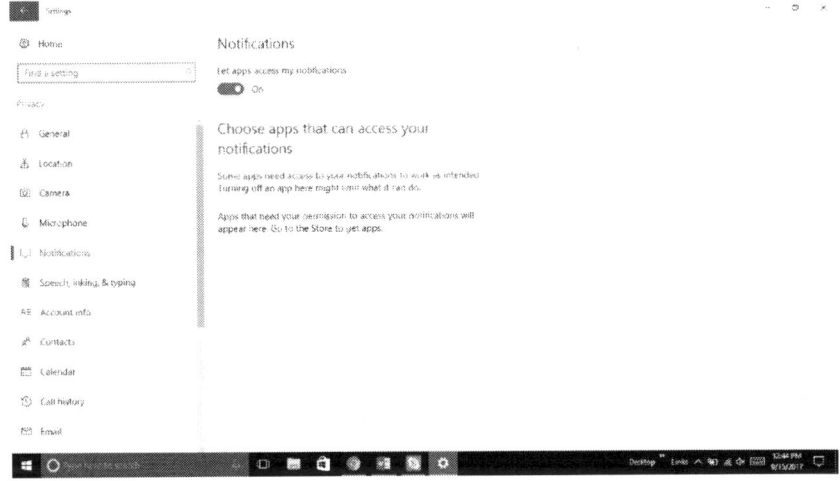

These are the major settings you should do away with immediately, for not only are they annoying, but they compromise security as well.

Keyboard shortcuts

One thing about Windows 10 is that you have A LOT of keyboard shortcuts. For some of us, we might not use this function that much. For others, it could be an integral part. So what are some of the shortcuts you can use? Well, read on to find out.

To select all of an item: Ctrl+A

To paste something: Ctrl+V or Shift+Insert

To open a new file to work in on any sort of Windows program: Ctrl+N

To cut something from a document: Ctrl+X

To copy something that you have: Ctrl+C

To close an app or window: ALT-F4

To delete a file permanently: Shift+Delete

To go between tabs and various Windows you have open: Alt+Tab

To open the start menu: Windows key

To go through the pinned apps: Windows key+T

To open a numbered app in a potion: Windows key+Alt+[number]

To minimize all Windows: Windows key+M

To restore any Windows you've got minimized: Windows key+Shift+M

To minimize all Windows but the ones that you're currently using: Windows key+home

To move to different virtual desktops: Windows key+CTRl+left arrow

To open the action center: Windows key+A

To go to Cortana text mode so you can type what Cortana should look for: Windows key+S

To have Cortana listen to what you say: Windows key+C. You can also just tell Cortana to listen

To open file explorer: Windows key+F

To go to the settings menu: Windows key+I

To lock your computer: Windows key+L

These various shortcuts will help with your experience, and for the ones you don't totally understand, we'll go over just what those do in the ensuing chapters.

Changing your personal info on Windows 10

If you're looking to change your personal info, such as the sig-in screen name in Windows 10, there are a few things that you can do in order to accomplish this. There are a lot of different options that you can change, and this section, will go over just how to do it.

Now, to change your sign-in name, you go to the Windows key+I to open settings, like said before. Then choose accounts>your email and accounts><manage my Microsoft account. You can then load the profile in your browser.

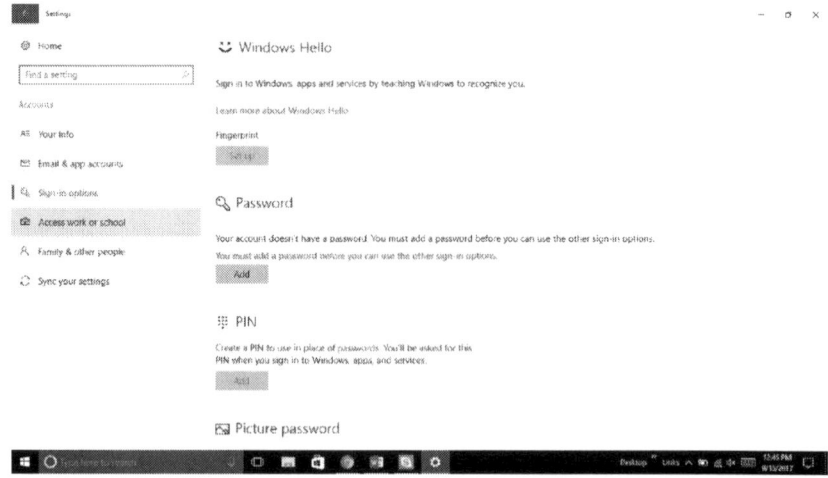

To change your name, you simply press the Edit Name tab. You can at this point change your name, the sign-in information that you need, whether you need a password or not, and other settings that you feel are necessary to enhance your Windows 10 experience. On the flip side, you can as well remove a password if you feel like you don't need it in order to have a great Windows experience.

At this point, you should then restart your computer. You'll notice the name change at the sign-in screen, and you should be able to use the password that you've created, but if it's still registering the old password, you might have to wait a bit.

You should also note that if you are going to do this, you'll need to as well change the name on outlook.com as well and other synched devices. That's because all of this is connected to the

Microsoft account.

For a local account, you don't have to sign in to your Microsoft account, since it's just an account that you have locally. You should open up the Power User menu by pressing Windows key+X and then choose control panel>change account type>choose your account>change account name/password/type of account/delete the account. You've got a lot of settings here. If you're simply looking to change your name, choose a new name, click "Change name" and it'll be complete.

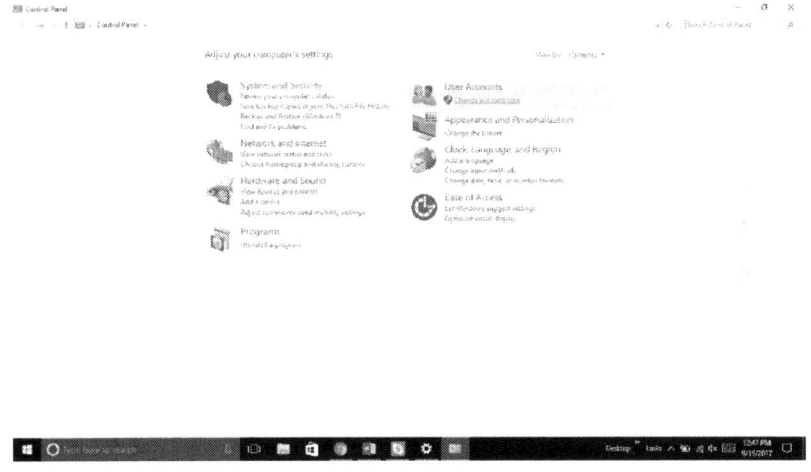

Changing your personal info on Windows 10 isn't that hard, and with the addition of various shortcuts as well, it makes the whole thing a lot simpler.

Changing screen resolution

Sometimes the screen resolution can look bad on the computer that you have. If you have a resolution that is too small and makes everything look blurry or too high and everything is tiny, you'll want to change it. Typically, these monitors run at a resolution of 800x600 or 1024x768. But for some computers that have LCD monitors or laptops that can handle the higher resolutions or require a specific resolution, you might want to consider this. Now, to increase this, it's actually pretty simple.

To do this, go to control panel>appearance and personalization>adjust screen resolution. Choose what you want, and then choose Apply and you'll be able to see how it looks. If it looks great, press Keep. If it looks bad, choose Revert to go back to what you have before. You'll definitely want to play around with this if you're not totally sure.

If you're stumped on what type of resolution to use, consult your device and see what the ideal specs are.

How to synch devices

Synching allows multiple devices to work with your Windows 10 that you have, so you don't have to repetitively put in the same settings. How do you do this?

Well first, you need to make sure the synch settings are on, and all of this is turned on, including themes. Go to start<settings<accounts<sign in. Sign in with your account, and then choose to Sync your Settings. Essentially, you do that with all Windows 10 machines, provided you have that turned on.

If you want to sync your phone, you'll have to download the OneDrive app to what you have, and then, you can link everything together. You can also just use a USB cable and choose to sync this from the menu as well.

How to upgrade from Windows 7 or 8

Now, you might want Windows 10, but fear the charge. However, there is a way to get around this. Really, you can go to "Windows 10 free upgrade for customers who use assistive technologies" and from there choose to upgrade. You'll see how to go through the setup process, and from there, it'll be on your device. It's that simple.

You don't have to worry too much about this, for it's quite easy to get around the system if you know what you're doing, but if you have Windows 7 or 8, it's best if you do upgrade to 10 so that you get the best results possible.

These are the first settings that you should know in order to obtain the best results from Windows 10. Try them, and see for yourself just how beneficial they are to your experience.

Chapter 2 – How to Customize Windows 10

For many of us using Windows 10, we want to have a custom experience. Many times, you might see some of the cool, neat backgrounds that people have, and themes that make you go "how did they get this?" You might want to learn, and you might even ask yourself this as you look at the screens. How do you do that? Well, you're about to find out, for this chapter, will tell you how to get all the fun custom additions that you want in Windows 10.

How to create custom shortcuts

For some of us, we want to have a different set of shortcuts that work better for us. Maybe we have a few specific settings that just worked killer for this, and we don't want to lose them. How do we fix this then? Well, you're about to find out.

You can first create a desktop shortcut by going to the

command prompt menu, choosing "Run as administrator" in the bar, and from there, type in "explorer shell: appsfolder" without the quotes around it, press enter, and that's where the apps are. From there, you can choose an app that's there, and choose the tab that says "create shortcut". If you have a lot of apps, you can change it to "detailed list" so you can see everything in one fell swoop. From there, choose the app you want. It'll ask if you want to create a shortcut to the desktop. Obviously, choose next. From there, right click on this icon and select "Properties." From this point, you want to choose the shortcut key field. All of this must be Ctrl+Alt+whatever letter or number you so desire to put in. From there choose okay. Don't use the same combination as well, since that'll confuse you.

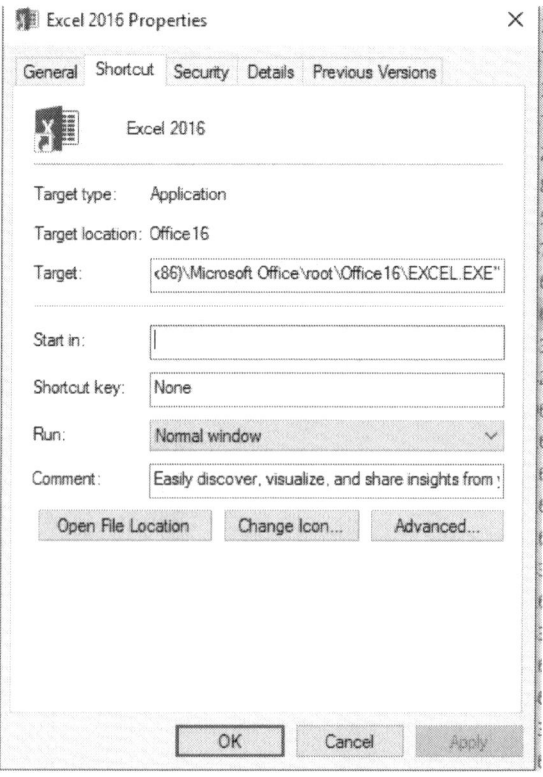

If you want a simpler way that creates it directly from the start menu, here is how. Go to start, choose the app that you want, from there choose open file location, go to properties again on this, and do the same thing that you did before.

Shortcuts are awesome especially if you need something opened up all the time. By doing this, you can make Windows 10 feel like your own, and you'll love it even more.

How to make Windows 10 feel like 7

Now, some people aren't super happy with the way Windows 10 looks. They want the old Windows back, especially if they loved 7. So how do you do this? Well, there are a few things that you can do.

Now, you can first install the classic shell version 4.2.2 since this is the only one that works with Windows 10. If you do this, make sure that you deselect classic explorer and IE, because let's face it, IE was never useful.

To get the classic start settings, you'll need to get classic shell running. See the icon in the right corner near the start menu. Choose settings, or choose classic start settings. Make sure that you choose to show all settings, choose the start menu style and go to the "Windows 7 style." Download it. If you really want the custom start button, you can then go to navigate the start button area from this same window, go to custom button, and you can then choose the image that you want.

Once finished, you should go to the Skin tab and then choose Windows Aero, and then press okay. Boom, you'll have the Windows 7 start menu.

To hide Cortana, you can right click the search box, go to the Cortana tab, and then choose "hidden."

If you for whatever reason hate the lock screen because it's slow and you have to click to get rid of it, but would like the Windows 7 screen once more, it's actually pretty simple. Go to Windows+R, type regedit, hit enter, go to **HKEY_LOCAL_MACHINE\SOFTWARE\Policies\Microsoft\Windows** in the box that you see. Right click on this right pane that you have. Choose New>key and you'll have a new folder added to it. That's a key. Write in personalization, select it, then right click and choose New>DWORD (32 bit value) on the right side of this. Rename it to NoLockScreen and from there, double click, set it to 1, and then click Ok to finish up.

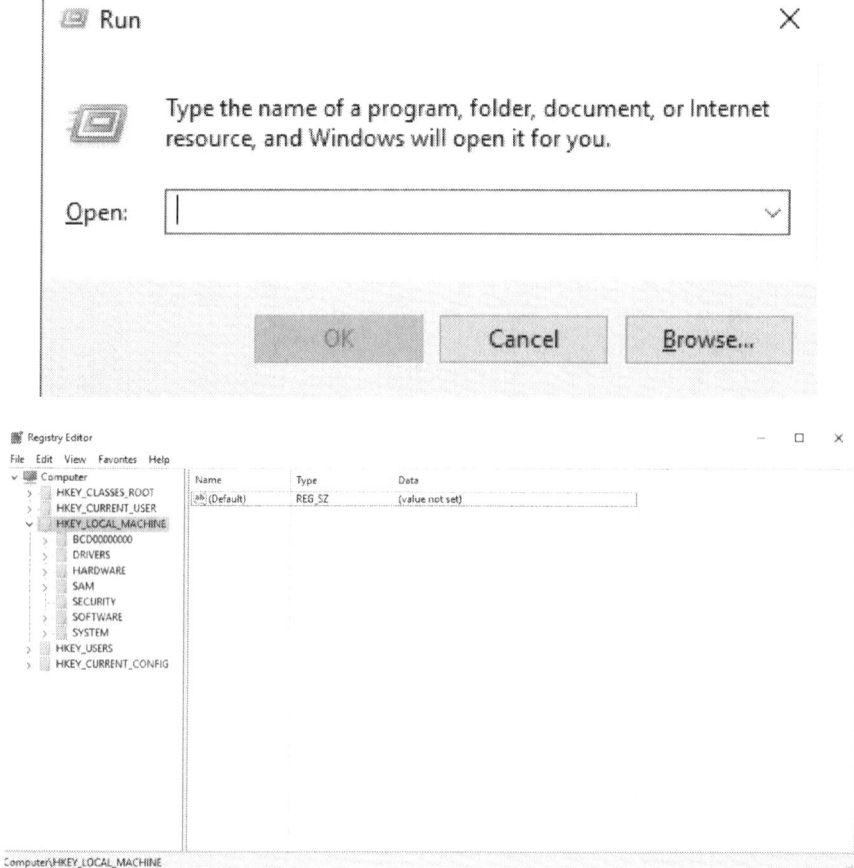

With all of this, you'll be able to get some neat Windows 10 settings set back to 7. This was a big problem at the beginning of this, but if you've wanted to change it but don't know how, then look no further.

How to change themes, backgrounds, and lock screens

Let's face it, the Windows 10 backgrounds and lock screens are kind of bland. The lock screen can be cool, but if you want something more personable, here's how you do it.

For background: you go to settings>personalization which is down on the list. Go to background at this point, choose the box underneath this to choose whether you want a picture, color, or slideshow on this. If you have lots of pictures, slideshows can be cool, and you can adjust how long you want a picture on there when you use this. There are a few that you can choose for your background, but if you have something saved on your computer, you can then choose it, and save that as your desktop background.

For the lock screen, it's virtually the same thing. You just have to go to the same menu in control panel, and from there, choose the lock screen one. You're essentially given the same things, and if you don't wat to use the custom ones that they give you, you can then proceed to upload your own as a result of this as well.

Now for themes, you can choose your own if you have a great one. To do this, you want to go to that same menu as you were at before. From there, you can right click a theme in order to save it. Give it a name, press Ok, and from there you can use it. You can then save it and share it with others if you have a nice one that you think others might like.

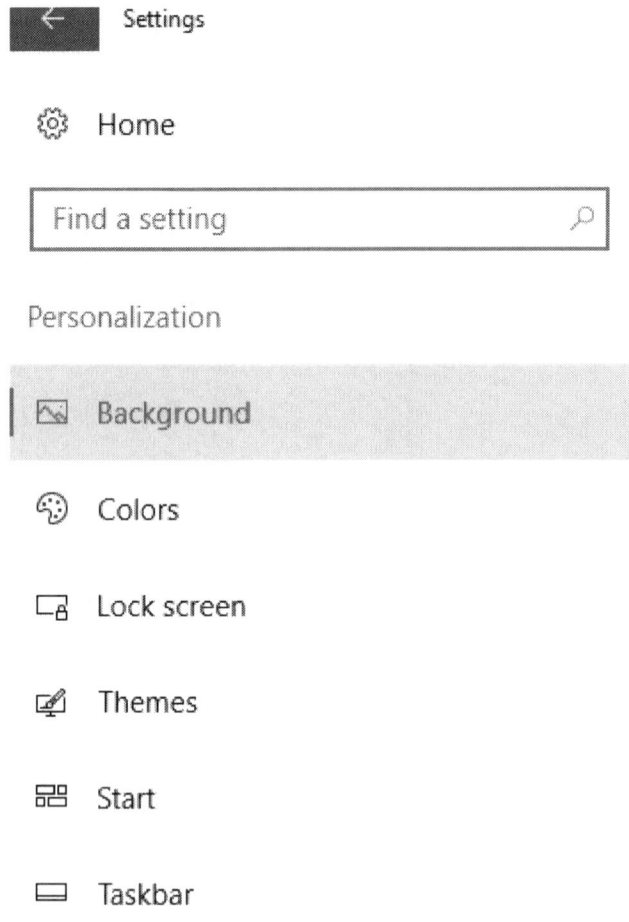

How to hide your name on lock screen

Sometimes, you don't want people knowing the name and email on the login screen. Fortunately, you can change this.

One of the methods is going to the "local group policy editor" in the task bar. Hit enter, and from there go to computer configuration>Windows settings>security settings>local policies>security options. You can double click on the icon that says, "interactive logon: display user information when the session is locked." Choose "do not display information" choose Ok to use this immediately and then choose "interactive logon: do not display last user name." Make sure that the setting is disabled, click ok, and then you're done.

How to edit photos to put in backgrounds

Now let's say that you have this great photo, but the resolution will make it look silly when you use it as a background. How do you get photos to fit to the Windows 10 screen? Well fortunately, you're about to find out.

First, choose the photo and hover over the top of this. Choose Edit>crop>aspect ratio>lock screen. You can then adjust it to the box as you need to by moving the various dots around in order to portion this, and then you can choose to apply this after that. You can then choose to save a copy of this. Now, to apply it right away, press the "…" button, choose set as>background/lock screen as necessary.

And there you have it, a picture that will fit the dimensions of Windows 10!

How to get classic games on Windows 10

Did you know that you can get the classic games such as solitaire and minesweeper on Windows 10? It's pretty awesome, and you might wonder how to do this. Fortunately, you're about to find out.

Now first you have to go to WinAero. Choose the "Download Windows 7 games for Windows 10, 8 and 8.1 zip." You will want the one that's next to the bullet point ones. Go past the ads, and click the link that's near the button that says "donate" choose to open with file explorer, and wait to download. You can then extract the files by double clicking this. Choose the application file that you need, and then choose yes when you're prompted to. You'll have to wait. They'll ask you for your language, and you can select English or whatever at this point. Press the next tab, choose what games you want, install them, wait for that to install, and there you have it, Windows 7 games installed on Windows 10!

These custom settings will allow you to get even more out of Windows 10. Try them, and see for yourself if this is indeed what you want, and if that is what you feel you need in order to have the best Windows experience.

Chapter 3 – Bugs and Annoyances and how to Solve Them

Installing Windows 10 can be quite great, but there are a few bugs and annoyances. You might wonder how you can resolve these. Fortunately, there are a few things that you can do in order to fix them. This chapter will go into just how to repair Windows 10 in an effective manner.

Repairing Windows 10

Why would you need to repair Windows 10? Well, sometimes it won't start, or it'll boot, but then it'll start to crash or run slow. This could be a sign that a virus has gotten into your computer, and you'll need to fix it fast. Fortunately, there is a means to, and you're about to learn how.

Typically, you'll want to use the Windows startup repair, especially if you can't even get to the login screen, or your desktop. Now, to get to this, you can go to the Windows 10 startup screen. Typically, hitting F11 is the easiest way. You can then go to troubleshoot, go to advanced options, and then click the tab that says startup repair. From there, Windows will start to fix the problems that it might have. If you don't have a problem, it'll say that it can't fix it, which means that there is something else going on here. Sometimes, you need to perform a full system restore of this. If you do so, you'll lose a lot of settings but it'll take you back to a specific time. You'll want to go to advanced options again, but this time choose system restore.

The computer will reboot, and you'll have to go from the beginning, including choosing your name, entering your password. If you have restore points, use this, if not, you can't do that.

Now, if you've got a corrupted file, it can also cause these problems. You might have to use safe mode if you can't get this going. You should check for these types of files though.

To begin, boot the computer, and go to the search box. Type in .cmd into there and then right click on the area that says, "command prompt" and choose "run as administrator." You will then have to type in **sfc /scannow** at this prompt, and from there, choose enter. It'll then scan for any corrupted files that might be there and restore them to the original settings.

Now, if you are totally unable to get anywhere with the above methods listed, it might mean that you'll have to do a hard reset of Windows 10. However, it will take your computer back to before you had any sorts of software, devices, or data that was loaded or downloaded. It is a good idea to do this before you give it to someone else so that everything is wiped.

Sometimes, you'll have to repair Windows 10, and here are a

few major troubleshooting options that you can choose in order to get the best results possible using Windows 10.

Fixing a slow download folder

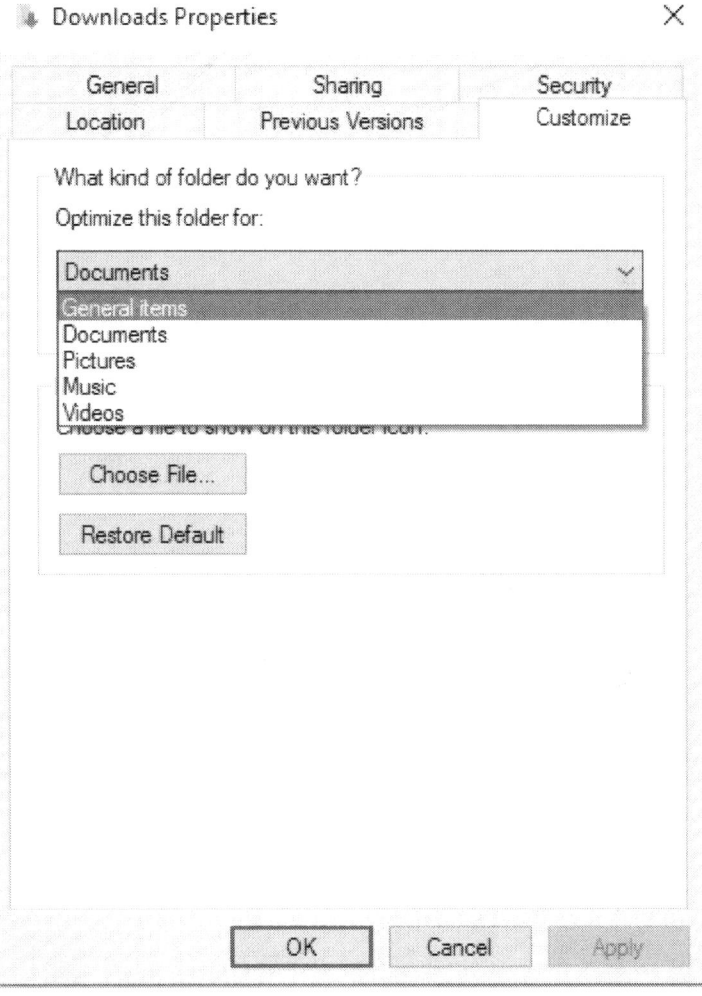

If you have downloads, sometimes it might take a couple seconds to pop up. But, if it's taking an abnormally long time, there might be something stopping it. Even if you have an SSD, if it's running at normal load times, that means that something is amiss, and you should immediately check out for this. How do you do that? Well, you're about to find out.

To do this, you open file explorer by pressing Windows key+ E or by going to the explorer icon if you don't want to use a shortcut. Go to the downloads shortcut, and right click the properties tab. Go to the customize tab, and select "general items" in the area that says, "optimize this folder for." Press ok and you should have a much speedier download drive from this.

Stopping updates

Now we've gone over how to stop the Windows 10 updates, but what about other apps. What about skype, which loves to update at times at the least opportune moments? Well, you're about to find out how to do this in a simple, yet effective manner.

To begin, launch skype if you already haven't.

Go to tools>options>go to the advanced tab>automatic updates. From here you can choose to "turn off automatic updates" with a push of the button." You might have already turned this off a long time ago, and if it says to turn it on, that means you've already done so. You should then save it.

Now, if you're going to use skype, I don't suggest doing this. It won't allow you to use the system, instead, update it when you're going to need it for best results.

Advanced startup options

We discussed earlier that you might need the advanced startup options menu if you have problems with the way your computer is running. If that is the case, here are a few means in order to help you get the most out of your startup options and how to access them.

First, try by hitting F11. This is the easiest one, and often, it's what people use to get to the menu. Do it as soon as you turn it on.

Now, you can boot it off an install disk. This can be on a USB or a DVD, and you can boot it to get to the advanced startup options menu. You should first create a bootable Windows 10 disk. From there, hit a button to boot it off and from there choose next, choose to repair your computer, and then press troubleshoot.

There are times where if you're constantly getting a startup error, you can go to the menu. That can happen automatically, and sometimes if you're not totally familiar, that's the best means to.

Finally, you should hit the restart button with the shift key held down.

Now, you first press the power button. Hold down shift, press restart, go to troubleshoot, and work from there by going to the advanced options menu.

Restarting Windows 10 without rebooting

Sometimes, we don't have the time or the patience to deal with Windows 10's constant updates. However, there are ways to restart without going through the full restart. You can have everything rebooted, and the updates will happen normally.

Press CTRL+ALT+Del in order to access the menu. Choose Task Manager, go to Windows explorer and from there, right click and select to restart this option. This will save you a boatload of time, and it'll make it a lot better for you too.

How to disable internet explorer

Now, Internet Explorer is still on all Windows 10 computer, it's just called Edge. If you really want it around, great. It's kind of a better version of IE, but compared to Firefox and Chrome, it's still lacking. However, you can get rid of it and completely disable it. Want to know how? Well keep on reading, and you'll find out.

To do this, right click the start button in the corner, choose control panel, go to programs, choose the one that says programs and features, and then in the left sidebar., you can then select to "Turn Windows features" either on or off. Now you should then make sure to uncheck the one that says Internet Explorer 11. Choose yes when asked, and this will ten completely disable this, making it so that you don't have to even look at this when using your computer. It's a feature that is still used, but it's one that can be quite annoying since sometimes, if you're working with a Microsoft app, it'll go straight to this.

How to pause updates.

Now if you just want to get rid of updates temporarily, then you can do just that. Sometimes, you might want to turn them off entirely, other times you just want it off for a little while. We'll tell you how to turn it off for just a little while, pausing the updates so that you don't have to deal with them.

Go to start>settings<update and security<advanced options<toggle the area that says, "pause updates" and choose to turn it on. As simple as that, you'll be able to reduce the clutter of updates, which in turn can be nice. Just remember that sometimes updating your computer is important and Windows 10 does get updates in order to make the system the best that it can be.

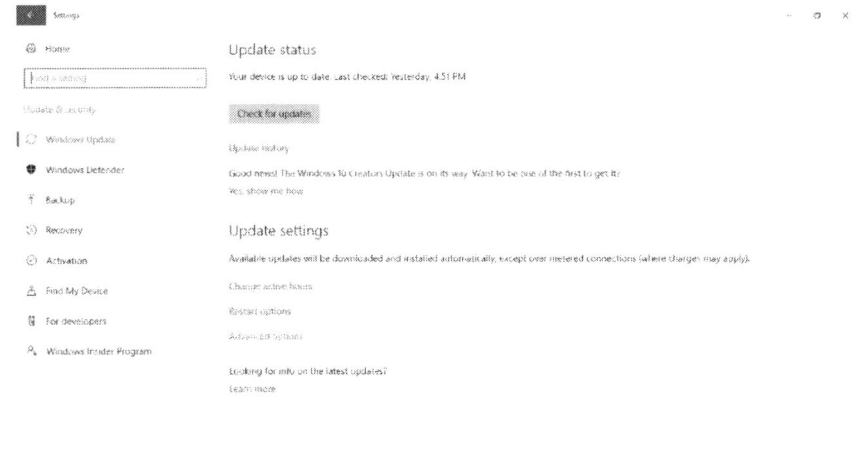

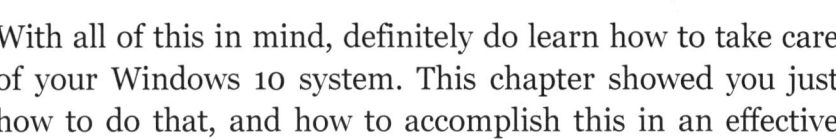

With all of this in mind, definitely do learn how to take care of your Windows 10 system. This chapter showed you just how to do that, and how to accomplish this in an effective manner.

Chapter 4 – What is Cortana and how to use it

For those of us new to using Windows 10, we might wonder how we can use Cortana. What is it though? What's the purpose of this? Well, you're about to find out in this chapter.

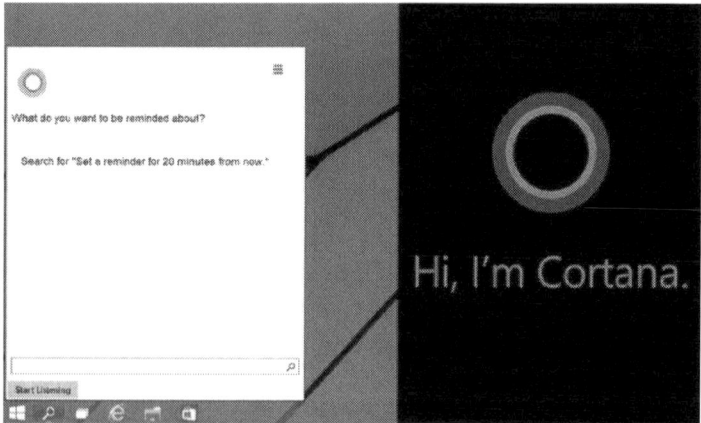

All about Cortana

If you've been keeping up with recent digital trends, the idea of an "assistant" to help you get somewhere with your computer is something that has recently taken the world by storm. From Siri, to Alexa, to Cortana, these navigators are great.

Cortana is essentially the Microsoft digital assistant, and the rule of thumb is that the more you use her, the better she will be for you, since it creates a way more personalized experience for the user that uses it.

Now, you simply talk to her or type something to her, and you'll then be given the answers. We'll discuss how you use Cortana exactly later on, but that's really the extent of it. If you don't know what to say to it, you can test it out by saying some suggestions you see when you open up the lock screen or even the Cortana home menu has a few grand ideas for this.

Cortana does a lot, including giving your reminders of what's going on, sending various texts and emails, creating a list for whatever you need, get information and facts on something, tracking everything from packages to sports teams to even flights, managing your schedule and calendar, keeping it up to date, giving you games to play, and even allowing you to open up any app that you have. Cortana does a lot, and it's one of the best things about the Windows 10 OS. It runs off this, and it is kind of the competitor to the Siri system.

How to use Cortana

To begin by using this, you can simply say "hey Cortana" and the system will respond. You can also open up Cortana by going to the taskbar and open up Cortana in the home menu. If you don't have it set already, go to settings>let Cortana respond to "hey Cortana" and make sure that's turned on. You can then start to speak to it. Now, it will need to know the speech, inking, and other patterns, so if you don't have that on yet, make sure you do. You also need to have your location on as well, since it'll use that location for all of the settings. If you are a bit worried about location sharing and such, then you might not want to use Cortana.

Now what can Cortana do? Well, it can help you with virtually anything. You can access I by going to the search feature in the taskbar area at the bottom of your computer. You can adjust this by either showing the Cortana icon or the search box, whatever works for you. You can also hide Cortana and still be active with it. However, once you click on the search box, it'll show up, and you can then look at your interests and hobbies associated with this.

You can also ask Cortana to do various tasks for you. Touch the notebook icon that's at the Edge of this, and you can then configure Cortana. Everything from finances, to eating and drinking, to even setting reminders and events, can be configured with the help of Cortana.

With Cortana, you can also change the name that Cortana uses to talk to you, how it's said, and it can also be used to edit the various places that are involved. You can save locations, and you'll be able to look at this to see what you can use.

How to navigate Cortana

Cortana has something called Google Cards, and these are suggestions that you can use with Cortana, along with some tips. These tips can involve anything from weather, traffic, and the like. You can look at these, or if you don't want them, you can simply go to settings to turn them off.

Now, each of these cards can be configured if you want to just have one on or one of them turned off. For example, you'll see the "eat &drink" card, and you'll be able to see food and drink recommendations. However, if you don't want that, you can simply turn it off, and that will suffice as well.

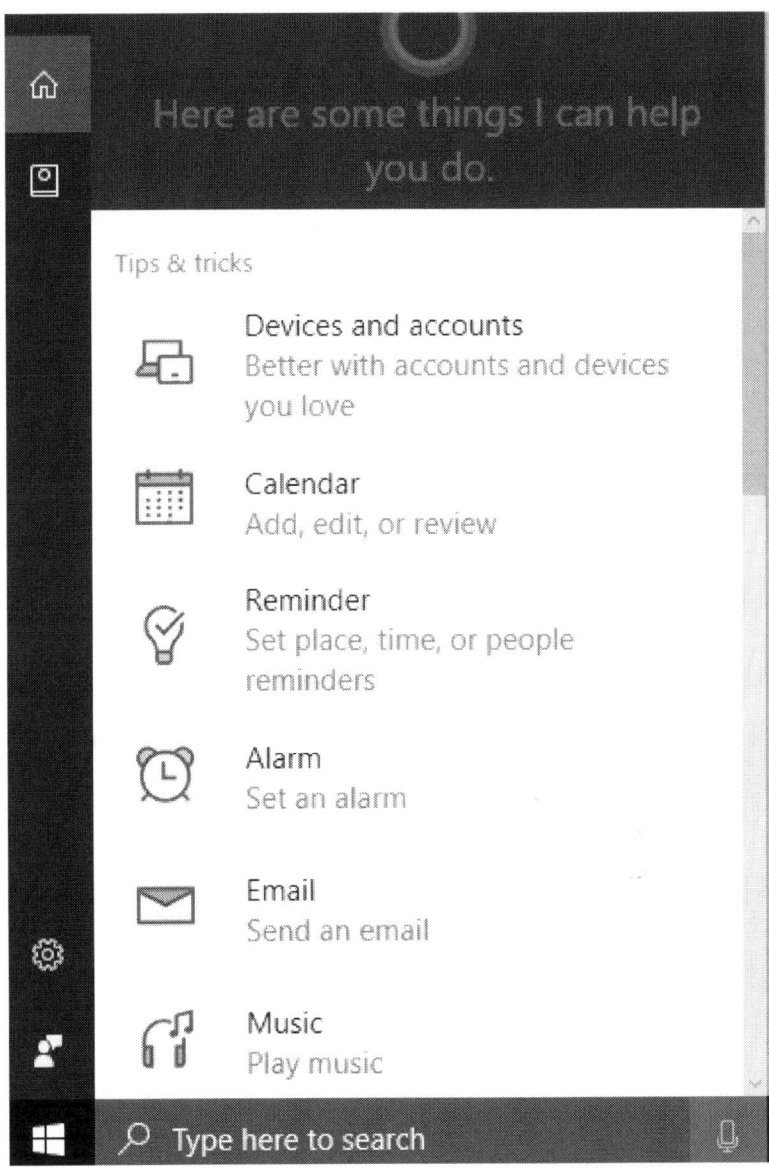

Reminders are another one that you can implement as well. Similar to what Siri and Alexa do, you can use Microsoft's Cortana in order to set various reminders, which you can adjust by the person it's about, the time it is, or even the location.

Finally, if you see that you want to send over some feedback to Microsoft on a bug, or if you want to give them feedback on how to make Cortana better during the next update, you can do this as well. You should ideally go through every single item that is here, including the cards that the notebook has, and you can start to configure it. Simply put a bit of the info that you feel is good for this, and from there, you'll be able to easily and without fail, use Cortana without any sorts of issues.

Removing Cortana

So let's say that while Cortana is great, you might not feel like you need it. This can be changed, and here is how. To do this, you want to go to the notebook tab. You'll notice immediately that the first thing you can do is turn it on and off, and it'll do just this. You might also want to turn off all of the privacy settings that you no longer need. If you don't want to use them, just simply turn off speech, inking, and typing. If you don't want to use the location, you can turn that off as well, depending on if that is necessary or not.

Now, if you're going to use Cortana, you should keep it around, but if you feel like Cortana is really just an invasion of privacy, which it might be depending on how much you use it, I do suggest that you turn it off. Again, this is your choice, since you are going to be giving Cortana a whole lot of personal information, which you might not enjoy.

If you're looking for a great personal assistant to your computer, you should definitely seek out Cortana. By doing this, you'll be able to use the system to your advantage, and you'll be able to achieve great success through the use of Cortana, and you'll be surprised at just how much this could end up helping you.

Chapter 5 – How to Enhance the Performance and the Productivity of Windows 10

Right now, you know of the basics of Windows 10, which is great, but if you want to know a bit more about it, it's time to learn how to enhance this. This chapter will go into the tons of ways you can enhance your Windows 10 experience, and how to do each one of these.

How to Speed up Windows 10

Let's face it, Windows 10 can be pretty slow, and you might not want to spend the time monkeying around with trying to pout Windows 7 or 8 on there. So how do you make this faster? Well, you're about to find out.

First, go to start>type power options>select the button that says that>choose the function that says, "choose what the power button does">select the button that says, "Change settings that are currently unavailable" if you notice that the shutdown settings are grayed out.

From here, you want to check the little tab that is nearby that says, "turn on fast startup." This will cut the time by about two-thirds. Obviously save this, and then you're on your way.

"God Mode" and how to activate it

God mode is something that you've been able to use in older Windows versions, but for 10, it's neatly hidden. You can activate it though, and we'll tell you just how to do this.

First, you need to go to your desktop, and from there, you want to right-click it to go to new>folder to make a new folder. Now at this point, you can name the folder *GodMode.{ED7BA470-8E54-465E-825C-99712043E01C}* with all of the brackets and the period put together. Now, if you don't want to call it God Mode. You can rename it various other cool commands such as Ninja Mode or Jedi Mode (no spaces obviously) and then you can open this up.

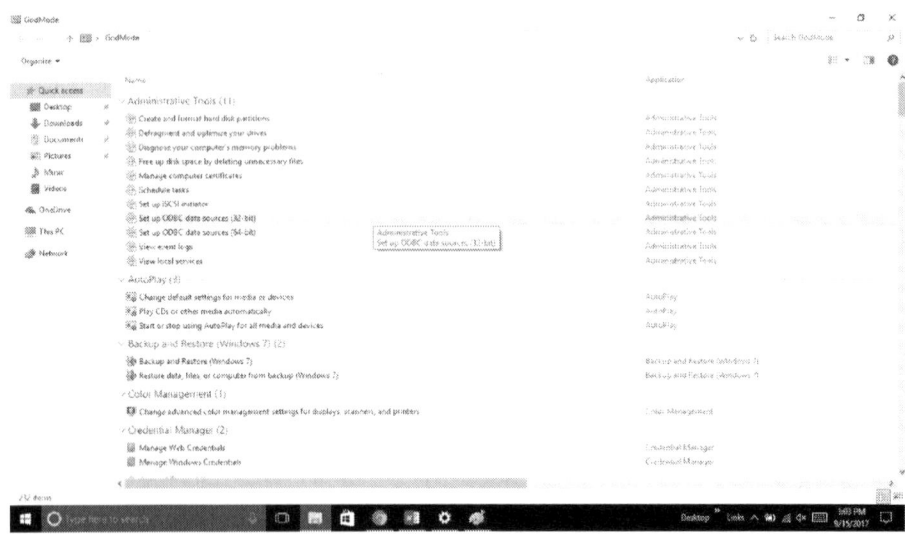

From here, you'll get over 260 various commands, such as options for administrative functions, internet options, and even backup tools. If you want to, you can always come back to this by leaving it on your desktop for added efficiency.

How to get the Superfast mouse

Sometimes we feel as if our mouse is too slow. You might want to move over and handle everything with just one general motion. If that's the case, here's how you can get that.

First, you need to make sure that your mouse speed is at the highest it can be. To make sure that it is, go to the control panel on Windows, go to the mouse menu, open the touchpad driver, and then change the pointer speed to max. From here, go to the pointer options tab that you see, and make sure that the pointer slider is all the way to the right side, and make sure to uncheck the button that says, "enhance pointer precision." Press Ok, and your speed will be even faster.

Now, to make this faster you have to go to the registry editor first. Simply press Windows+R to get there, enter in regedit, and press enter.

You want to go to the navigation pane and press **HKEY_CURRENT_USER\Control Panel\Mouse** and from there, go to mouse speed and press the 2 button. Put the first mouse threshold to 1 and the second to 0, and then you can simply close and reboot. There you have it, a super-fast mouse.

How to mirror your screen to another monitor or TV

Now, if you're someone that wants to mirror your computer to another, for the purposes of streaming, you can certainly do so. For this, you'll need a Miracast receiver, which are pretty easy to get, and a TV set. You can't use a Roku box with Microsoft devices, so it's best you avoid this. However, the Microsoft wireless display adaptor is one of the best for this.

Now, to begin, set this up and make sure you're got everything plugged into your TV and set up.

From here, go to start>settings>devices>connected devices>add a device>choose the receiver that you have.

That's all you have to do. At this point, it should be mirrored over to where your television is. If you can't, repeat it, but sometimes, you might just have a bad miracast device, so do look at it.

Now, to disconnect this, you want to go to your receiving device that's under the Projectors tab in the Devices section. You choose a device, press yes to remove this, and then there you go. That's all you need to do.

How to get the most out of your CPU

One thing that's quite annoying about Windows 10 is how much it's a glutton for the CPU that you have. It will start to eat at it, and it has a bad habit of maxing that out. Now, this isn't the best way to run the computer, due to the fact that it ca overheat your computer, but if you need it to get some extra CPU into your device, then here's how you do it.

First, go to control panel, and then go to hardware and sounds. From there, go to power options, from there you should go look for the processor power management. You'll want to from here open the menu for the minimum processor state. You'll need to then change the settings on the battery to 100%. Make sure as well to change the plugged in % then to 100 as well. You can then close, reboot, and ten that's it. That's all you need to do in order to maximize that. You'll be able to truly get the most out of this if you try that.

How to record videos of various apps

One thing that many Windows 10 users don't know about, is the fact that Windows 10 does have a hiding screen device to record video in any sort of app. If you are looking to show how to do a tutorial on a Windows app, or you want to show off a bit of game streaming, you sure can. It's pretty easy to do this, and you'll be able to get a good, basic screen recording to show to others.

Now, you'll want to open up the app you feel like recording. There are a few that you can't record such as the desktop itself and the file manager, probably for a good reason, but if you're using normal apps from the Windows store or the desktop, you'll be able to open it.

Press Windows+G in order to open the Game Bar box. They'll ask you if this is a game. Say yes, and you'll be able to record what's on the app screen, whether you're recording a game or not. Obviously, if you want to record a game, you can do just that.

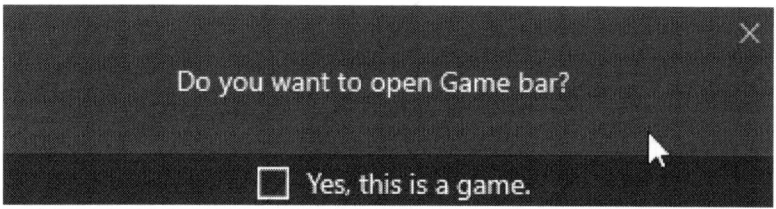

To start recording, you want to press Win+Alt+R in order to start capturing video. Now, to record this, you simply press the red recording bar that you see at the top right. You can press Win+G in order to bring the bar back. From there, you'll have a video of your app, and you can use this to share it with others, allowing you to have the best experience with this that you can have.

How to create a file for registry hacks

Now, the Registry is where you do configure some of the more advanced settings, from stopping the use of Edge to also enhancing your mouse speeds. However, this does take a long time, and it's super risky. It's best if you don't do this unless you truly need to. You can create a new registry folder to help save your changes, and you'll be able to do it with these steps.

First, you want to open up the registry editor by pressing Windows+R, type into the box regedit, and then press Ok.

Go to the registry value or the key, and then choose it. You'll start to notice that the folders are basically keys and the values are what are in the folders. You can copy one of these by choosing it, and pressing Ctrl+C to copy this.

Now, if you've already done this, you can go to the file menu at the top left, choose to export it, name this file, and then save this with a .reg extension for anyone who uses it.

Now, you can use this as well for whenever you want to give some computer a feature. For example, if you have five computers, and you don't want any of them to have the lock screen, that's how you do it, for you'll be able to export all of this to the computers, and it's that simple.

How to open stuff in the task bar

For those of us that don't like having to clutter the display that we have with a bunch of Windows, you can actually embed some of the folders that you need straight into the task bar. This is good for if you're working with a lot of folders and don't feel like sifting through the directories.

How do you do this though? Well to begin, right-click on any space that you're not using. Choose toolbars, choose from there a new toolbar, and then, go to the directory and folder that you want, you can then open up the folder straight from the task bar, choose what you're using, and then plug it straight into the area. This is good if you're sifting through and trying to find various directories that might take forever, or if you need a specific folder that's cluttered on your device.

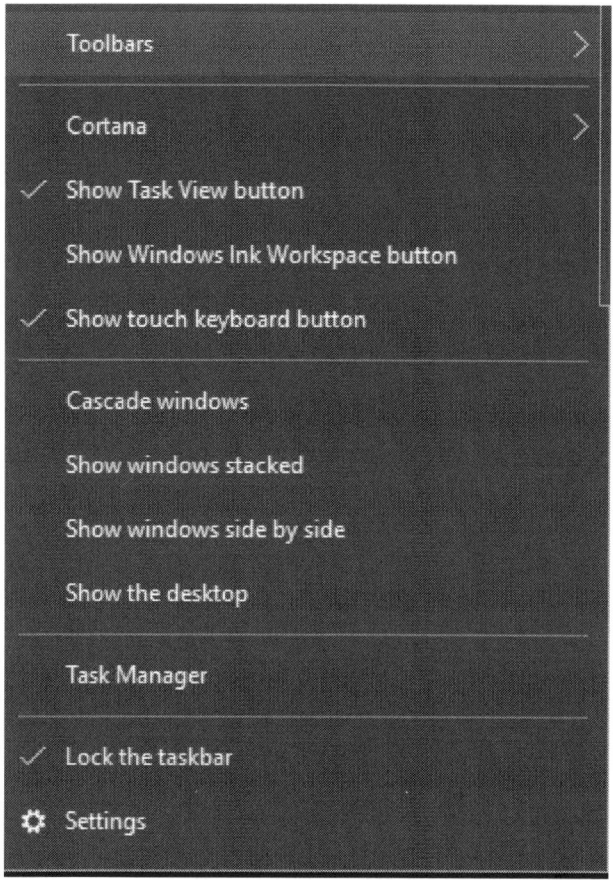

Along with this, we want to talk about websites too. Now, this is something that's kind of not seemingly a huge deal, but if you think about it, it'll save you a lot of various clicks, and you'll be able to open it right away. Here's how you do it.

Start with going to the unused space that's on the task bar, go to toolbars, but instead, go to address this time. You want to put the address into there, and ten press the enter key. You can then open up the pages in the default web browser that you have, which might be Edge if you haven't set chrome as the default. You can then also click the down arrow to look through the history with this website in order to find what you're looking for.

When it comes to making your computer the best that it can be, it might seem really complicated. It's not though, and these settings could save you a ton of time. With this chapter, you've learned how to effectively and without fail turn your computer into the best system that it can be, and you'll also be able to from here be able to open up whatever it is that you need to, enhancing the experience with Windows 10. With some of these, it might be best to wait until you've learned the basics, since it could end up creating problems later on.

Chapter 6 – Ways to Store Various Files on Windows 10

Storing with Windows 10 is pretty neat, since there are many ways to configure this sort of thing. This chapter will tell you just how to store some of the files that you have on Windows 10, and how to use OneDrive in order to keep everything in one Cloud storage place.

How to shrink Windows 10 to improve drive space

Windows 10 is a huge system, and it can take out a lot of disk space on your hard drive. Here's how you can shrink it so that the unnecessary files and such don't take up a ton of space on it for much longer.

First, go to settings, click on the file that says system, go to storage and then select the C: drive. That's your computer. Go to apps &features, and from there you'll see a lot of various apps that you more than likely don't need. Choose the one that you need, and then uninstall this.

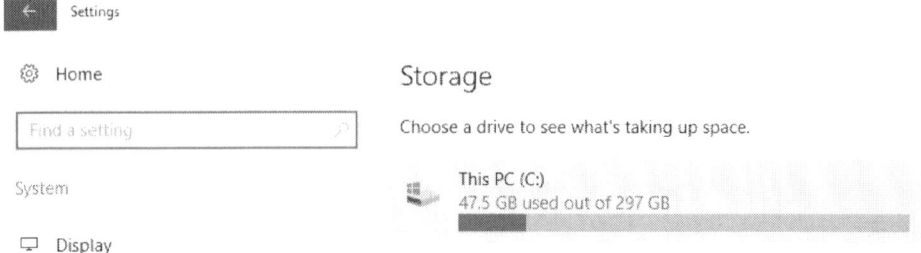

There are a few that you'll need to uninstall from other different areas, and if that is the case, you'll need to go there. But, most Windows 10 functions can be uninstalled from there.

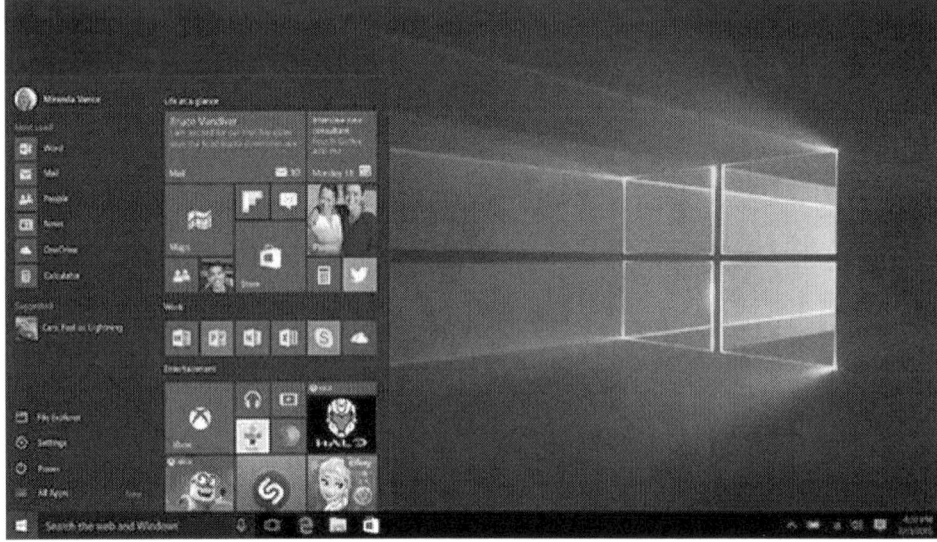

Hibernation is another culprit here. When you hibernate your computer, everything that's currently there gets saved. This includes the various documents and programs. You can disable it and save a lot of storage space. To do this, go to the Windows start button and open a command prompt in administrator mode, choose yes to open the command prompt and then in this window type in the following: **powercfg -h off** and then press the Enter key. This in turn will delete the hibernation files and remove the option that you might have to hibernate your computer. You can however, still put your computer to sleep, which will save the state of the computer to the memory versus the hard drive and keeps the computer on, but in a much lower power level.

Other ways to save space

There are a few other ways to save space, and you'd be surprised at how you can. This section will tell you of a few ways to save space on Windows 10, and why you should.

The first is you'll want to go and look for the old updates in the WinSxS folder, since these aren't needed. You can clean up the disk for the updates that you don't need.

Now, how to get there is to use the disk cleanup in order to get the older updates. You can go to the taskbar and type in the words "disk cleanup" and then click on it when it shows up. Press the button that says, "cleanup system files" and make sure you check the button that says, "Windows update cleanup" which will clean up the excess updates that you have here.

Now, if you want to look at the space that the SxS folder is accumulating so that you can get rid of what you don't need, you can use the command prompt.

To do this, you right click the Windows button and then click the area that says, "command prompt (admin)" in order to launch the command prompt. From there, when you do open this, type in ***Disme.xe*** ***/online*** ***/Cleanup-Image /StartComponentCleanup*** as written, and you'll be able to analyze the entire folder that you have and you'll be able to see if it's worth the cleanup. If you're unsure of if you should clean up a file, use your discretion on this.

Now, another location where space might be taken up is in the areas where you have large files that are totally unnecessary. These tend to hide in the storage drive, and they take up a ton of space. They're typically under names that seem like they're nothing, but they are actually quite large. How do you find it? Well, here is how.

Open up the file explorer; press the area that says, "this PC" and you'll see everything on the PC. Now go to the size tab and check for the ones that say that they are Gigantic, usually greater than 128 MB. These are huge, and you might have to wait a bit for the file explorer to show everything. You can then wait until everything is finished before you see what is just taking up everything. You can also simply look at the Local Disk C in order to simply look at the computer hard drive itself.

You'll want to press the details button that's located under the view tab, go to the size button that's on the right side next to the folder, and from there, look through and sift through to figure out what you don't need. Now, you should be careful about this. Only delete stuff that you know what it does, and you don't need it. A common mistake people make when they do this is they will erase very important files. You should always look up something you're not sure of.

Typically, ISO files, temp files, and program installers are all things that you can erase, so if you want to, you can do those, and then look up the rest of the file types as needed.

You should also go to the downloads folder. Lots of us will

download stuff, forget that we did, and then it sits on the file explorer collecting dust, and using up space. Luckily, you simply go through, and you do the same thing. You can go from largest to smallest, but usually, if you've downloaded a file for work, and you do not really need this, and then just get rid of this.

Alternatively, you can also save space by doing a thorough disk cleanup. You can launch it, select the C drive, agree to it by pressing Ok, from there, wait while it scans and then delete what you need to. Now, you can get rid of files in this way, especially temporary files, since these can take up a ton of space. Once finished, you press Ok, agree to delete the files, and when it's done, launch it again, select your D drive and then clean up the system files this time. Choose the C drive once more, and from there check off any files that you do need. Now, once you've decided that, the disk cleanup will get rid of all of the files that are unchecked. If you need a temporary internet file, do make sure it's left unchecked.

How to put Windows 10 apps onto an SD card

Now, most computers only have 32 GB of internal storage, and Windows 10 takes up a ton of this. You can however, put this onto a USB drive or SD card, and here is how.

First, put this storage device into your computer. I would suggest an SD card because it won't accidentally get knocked out and ruined like a flash drive might.

Go to settings>system>storage>new apps to save to>the SD card that you have>apply. That's as simple as it is, and you can then put everything from Windows 10 onto that for extra storage.

Now, if you already have apps and such installed, and you want to get them off your internal storage, here is how you do this.

First, go to settings>system>apps and features. From there, you simply press the move button, and you'll then be asked to verify where it'll go. Typically, the USB drive or the SD card will show up, and from there, you can move this over to there.

That's how you do it, and it's so simple, but saves a ton of space.

How to use Zip Files on Windows 10

Sometimes, we have a lot of files and we want to compress them. This is especially good if you're sending over documents and pictures that are huge in terms of MB. This will also save you a lot of memory on your hard drive as well.

Now to do this, you want to choose the files that you're going to compress first. If you just want to zip a file and nothing more, you don't have to do much, just choose it. To get all of the files together, you want to then click the main one, hold down the Ctrl key and then choose the folders that you want. Keep this held down until you're finished. Then, right-click this, and then choose "send to and select compressed" folder. Name the file, and there you have it.

Some people like to use the Ribbon menu, which is fine, especially if you're using a laptop that has a touch function rather than a right-click function. To use this, obviously have it in the ribbon menu.

Choose the files and folders you want, go to the share tab, press the zip button, and you can then add to this. You can then select the ones that you want, and put them as well into a zip file.

OneDrive and how to use it

OneDrive is a pretty name for one of the best features of the Windows 10 system. This is remote file access, and with this, you can grab a file from any computer, even if it's not on the OneDrive folder. If you're working with a lot of computers, you need to have this on, but how do you enable it? Well fortunately, you're about to find out. You want to turn on the fetching for this.

To do this, right-click the OneDrive icon and choose the settings function. Open it, and check the dialogue box that reads, "let me use OneDrive to obtain my folders on this PC." You will notice when you open this that it's unchecked. That's a default setting. Press Ok, and then right click on the icon once again, exit it, and let it restart. You can launch OneDrive and select the service that you need.

Now, if you need a file with OneDrive, first you need to make sure that you're logged into **https://onedrive.live.com/** on said computer. Click on the settings at the top left, choose Pcs, and then, click on it to look at the computers that you have, and then look at the computer you want to get to. You need to make sure that they're all listed under one OneDrive account. You'll need to sign into it with a security code, especially if it's your first time doing this sort of thing. You can then go through and look at the files that you have on the PC itself, including the ones that aren't even a part of your OneDrive. This is something that can be really helpful, and alternatively, it can really save the day if you're not careful.

These tips will allow you to save yourself a ton of space using Windows 10. You'll have a much more efficient computer, and one that works better as well.

Chapter 7: File Explorer Tips

The file explorer is a great tool, and you've learned a lot about it already. There are a few things that you can add to your repertoire of this, and here they are.

Changing the Windows Default Folder

When you open the file explorer, typically it either says Quick Access or This PC, and this is dependent on what your settings are. However, if you want it to run a different folder, opening a totally different one than before, here is what you do.

To begin, you want to right click on the desktop in order to get to the New tab, and from there, open up the Shortcut tab. It'll then give you the option to name the shortcut, which you should put in **C:\Windows\explorere.xe** into the bar. Press Next, and then name what the shortcut should be. You can always leave it as well if you so desire.

Press finish, and then when you get to the shortcut, go to properties. You should then go to the target area, and in that space, fill in **C:\Windows\explorere.xe /n,/e, [folder location]** which is the name of the folder that you want to open obviously. You can also put in some subfolders as well. When decided, you can then press Ok, and every time you use that shortcut, you'll be able to open up the folder that you need, instead of just the default file explorer folder, and there isn't a limit to how many you can throw on there as well.

How to Add the Control Panel to File Explorer

You can also add the control panel to this as well, which in turn will allow you to access the control panel area. It's a bit more involved however, but still very doable.

To begin, open the registry editor as we've said before. You then press enter, and then click yes in order to allow the registry editor to be used so that you can make changes to the device that you have. What you want to go to is the following: **HKEY_LOCAL_MACHINE\SOFTWARE\Microsoft\Windows\CurrentVersion\Explorer\MyCom** and then you want to create a name inside of this. You should right click the namespace key that is there, then choose new>key. Now, depending on the name, you could have the control panel open in either the view of the category or the icon. We'll tell you what you should put in for each one, below.

To name the control panel with category view, put in the following: {26EE0668-A00A-44D7-9371-BEB064C98683}

If you want to put in the icon view, add in the following: {21EC2020-3AEA-1069-A2DD-08002B30309D}

And there you have it, the exact means to use this in order to put the control panel onto the file explorer using Windows 10.

Disabling Quick Access

Quick access is a very efficient means to get to what recent files that you need. However, let's say you're using a shared computer, or one that is much more public. You might not want everyone to see all of the files that you have, and this is usually what will open as the default when you open up file explorer. So, with that in mind, let's talk about how you can disable this from file explorer.

To begin, go to file explorer from the start menu. Or, if you have it in the taskbar, go from there. You can click view at this point. Go to options, and then choose the area that says change folder, and then go to search options. From here, you'll want to get to the general tab, and then drop down to what says, "change the selection from quick access to this PC." Press Ok to close this. From here, you'll not be able to open up the file explorer in order to access what you need to, and you'll start to realize that you won't have to worry about people seeing anything the second you open up the quick access. You might not need this unless you're on a shared computer, but remember, sometimes it's better to be safe with these kinds of things.

Pinning the File Explorer to the Start Menu

For those of us that use the file explorer like it's going out of style, you'll want to pin this. Think about it, having to go through the motions of trying to open this up each and every time can be quite annoying, especially if you're someone that uses this function quite a lot. Luckily, the way to pin this is quite easy, and you'll be able to learn how to do this in just a couple of steps.

First, right click the taskbar in order to show it. From there, you go to desktop, and then, you can go to the various files that you need. You can access files in this manner.

In some cases, this is automatically pinned to the taskbar, which makes it easier for some of us, so we don't have to go searching around for this.

If you want to put it into the start menu, if that's how you can easily access it, first you want to open the file explorer, navigate to the folder that says Users on it. Go to the folder that you need. Choose the searches function. From there, you want to right click the right saved search that you have. You can then press the option that says, "pin to start" in order to pin this straight to the start bar.

When it comes to the file explorer, there is a lot that you can do with it, and this chapter showed just what sort of extent that you can use this with, and some of the cool, efficient ways to really improve your Windows 10 experience, and how to definitely get the most out of something like this.

Chapter 8: Cool Tips to Make Your Windows 10 Experience Easier

You've learned a whole lot about Windows 10. Now, it's time to learn some of the hacks that will make this system even easier. For those of us that know about how to do the basics, but want to know a few extra tidbits that will make this even better for you, then look no further. There are a few tips that will help with navigation, and you'll be able to improve and learn from this as well.

If you need to have a ton of tabs open, one of the best trucks to help with the clutter of this, is to move them left and right. Do this with the most front one that you have, and it'll allow you to look at every single tab. Then, once you're done, you can move it to the left and right, pick up your next one, and do the same thing.

The Start Manu Customizations

With the start menu, we discussed how you can pin some of the various aspects that you need straight to it, but if you want to change the size of the tiles, you can even do so now. Now, you can do this by going to the tiles of what shows up on the start menu, and you'll be able to go to the sizing option, and choose to make them bigger, or even smaller as well. You can put the programs there as well and also unpin them too. You can hold down the tile on a touch screen as well.

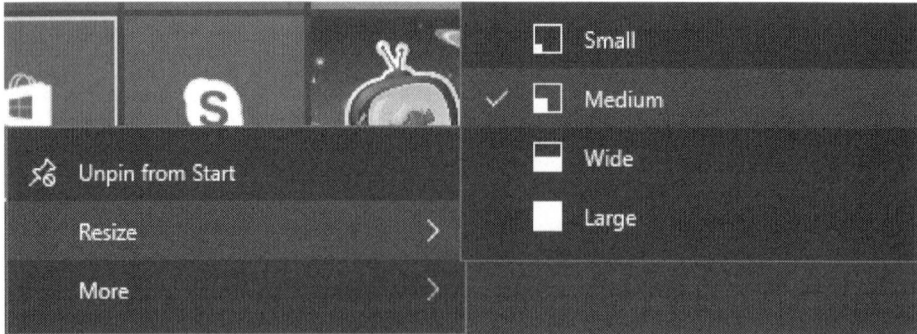

Now, live tiles are basically allowing you to go to anything on the computer without leaving the desktop. This can get quite annoying, and they constantly update. You can choose the option to "Turn the live tile of" by selecting it, and then you're finished. This is a neat little option if you're not interested in dealing with all of this.

Virtual desktops

For those that like to have multiple desktops, on a Windows 10 PC, this can be one of the best things. If you're someone that has a lot of office documents, or apps in general, the virtual desktops will allow you to completely organize this. You can choose the virtual desktop icon or go to Windows+Tab to see the Windows. The virtual desktop icon is the one nest to Cortana, if you're looking for it. You can then go to the right-hand side of this and look at the new option that will give you to have a new desktop. Simply click on it, and then you'll have it.

Navigation of Windows 10

If you're using a computer that has the touch function, one thing that you'll notice is that you can move your fingers about to navigate this. This can be quite jarring if you don't know how to use it. Fortunately, that is the case, and you'll be able to use this on the precision tablets that you have.

To see a task, slide the finger up.

To show your desktop, slide three fingers down.

To go to a previous app, you want to flick your three fingers to the left or the right.

To search for an app, simply tap the area with the three fingers that you have.

Now remember, this only works with precision laptops. You can go to settings>change PC settings>devices and Pc>touchpad and mouse. To tell if you have this or not, you should be able to see something called "Your PC has a precision touchpad."

When you go to the task view, that basically means that all of the Windows will be open, which in turn will allow you to see everything that you have, and to navigate through all of the virtual desktops.

Tablet mode

Who remembers Windows 8? You probably came from Windows 8 in some cases, but it was a system that few and far between truly enjoyed, however, one of the cool things about this was the touch UI that Microsoft had. However, this was kind of pushed to the side when it first came out. Now, with the advent and popularity of tablets, you can have the tablet mode back once again, and it will allow you to use this with any hybrid and precision devices.

Now, to go to this, you want to go to the notifications icon that you see in the taskbar. This is at the very right, and it looks like when you get a text message. You can swipe right if you're using the touch screen mode. You can then at the taskbar go to the action center. Then, you'll want to go all the way down to what says, "tablet mode" and from there, you can turn it on and off, and then, you'll need to restart to have it work.

You can also access this from the settings menu as well, but this is to permanently put it into there. It's best to make sure that you do like this before you choose to, for you'll have to go through this if you want to change out of this. You first have to go to settings, and then, go to the tablet mode option, and then, you can go to the drop down menu, and you can choose for it to show up "when I sign in." When you do click on this, you'll be able to boot it up whenever you last used it. You can then automatically switch to tablet and desktop move each and every single time.

Playing Xbox One Games

Now, obviously Microsoft is in charge of not only Windows, but also the Xbox system. If you have an Xbox one, you're in luck, because Windows 10 allows you to actually mirror the console onto your laptop and desktop. Not only that, you can stream, screen capture with this, and it can even rival the way the PS4 and the PS Vita stream, and it's arguably a better system than both of these.

Now, it's not that hard to do. You might wonder if it's complicated will take a while, or the like, but the easiest way to do this is for you to go to the Xbox app that's on your PC. You should make sure that your console is connected to Wi-Fi or else this won't work. From there, you should tap the symbol that appears on your PC, and from there, this will then show up.

Now, as of note, it can be a bit laggy if you're playing something that you know runs at super high settings. For example, it might not be advised to play Call of Duty on this. But, for those that are way slower-paced, that don't require a lot to run them, this is actually a pretty awesome way to stream and show off various aspects of a game on your PC.

You can also use the same app screenshot and streaming capture as we said before to help capture some of the content that you want to showcase to other people. This is great for those considering game streaming, for it does work quite well in this case.

P2P Updates

Probably one of the most annoying things about Windows 10 is the updates. We talked about this. However, if you want to control these and make sure that they're locked in at the right time, there are ways to do this. Now, the first thing you want to do is to open up the start menu, then head towards settings, click on the area that says updates and recovery, and then choose the option that says, "notify to schedule restart." Which will allow you to schedule the restart updates as well.

Now, you will at this point be able to get faster updates. You can use P2P tech in order to do this. Now, what you want to do is go to advanced options, and then choose how you get the updates. You can choose the updates from one place, turn it on, and make sure that you don't suck it up with all the bandwidth, which we'll discuss next.

How to update without Sucking up Bandwidth

Now, if you want faster updates, but don't want you to lose your bandwidth for the month, there are a few things that you can do. You should definitely try to optimize the delivery updates, and you'll be able to use the P2P network to help get them in a much faster manner. However, if you don't want to share the bandwidth, you can still get the updates super-fast.

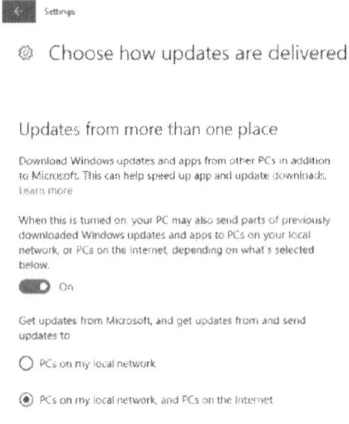

First, to disable it, you want to choose the settings menu, then go to update and security under the update tab. Click on advanced options, and then choose the button that says, "choose how updates are delivered." From here, you should now see the option to determine whether the updates are from "PCs in my local network" or "PCs on my local network and Pcs on the internet. If you want to have bandwidth more than the updates, go former. If you want faster updates but with the potential to sacrifice bandwidth still, go latter. You can then update all of the computers at home without having to download an update all the time. Obviously, keep your bandwidth in mind if you're going to do either of these.

Doodle Fun!

Finally, we have the doodle option that you can use on the Edge browser, probably one of the best options for the Edge browser. You can tap the icon hat has the pen and paper, choose what you're going to use, and then begin to doodle. You can then hold the pen in different manners, and it can change the hues of the pen, along with the sizes. You can from there, copy parts of this page too, saving it to OneNote. If you're using this in order to take notes, you can certainly save a copy, and it'll almost be like notetaking.

Obviously with this, do keep in mind that it only works with the Edge browser, which is not really used by many people, so it might not necessarily be a valuable function, but a function you can consider using.

These cool tips will allow you to make the most out of your Windows 10 experience. Try them, see what you can get from them, and learn about the various hacks that can make your experience better. Remember, all of these are quite optional, and you might not even need to use them. But, it's good to know just what extent Windows 10 can do for you, some of the valuable functions of it, and the extent that this system has for you as a user of it as well.

Conclusion

From this book, you've learned everything that you need to know to have a basic understanding of Windows 10. It's important to have the basics down pat, because even those that are seasoned with these computer systems might not even know of some of the hacks to make Windows 10 the best system that it can be. It can be quite complicated, and you might wonder how you can make this easier. Well, the truest, most surefire say to have the best experience possible, is to start by working with this, learning the system, and mastering it.

Which is what you should do next. Take your time, sit down with this, and learn how to utilize Windows 10 to your own personal advantage. Work towards being the best Windows 10 user you can be. For some of the more complicated functions, such as registry edits and such, it might be best to work with this once you've monkeyed around with a few of the other functions, but it is to your advantage to learn about this, to get an understanding for it, and to feel for all that you're doing.

So yes, sit down and work with Windows 10. Learn this system, use it to your advantage, and see what kind of a difference you can make. Remember, learning how to use this might seem so simple, so silly, but if you think about it, you probably didn't know half of the functions in here, so it's best to have a better idea of just what you're getting into, and how to use this. Lots of times people criticize Windows 10, but often, it's because they don't know it, and this book gave you the told you need to help get the most out of it.

I hope that you really enjoyed reading my book. If you want to help me to produce more materials like this, then **please leave a positive review on Amazon.**

Thanks for buying the book anyway!

I think next books will also be interesting for you:

<u>Amazon Customer Service</u>

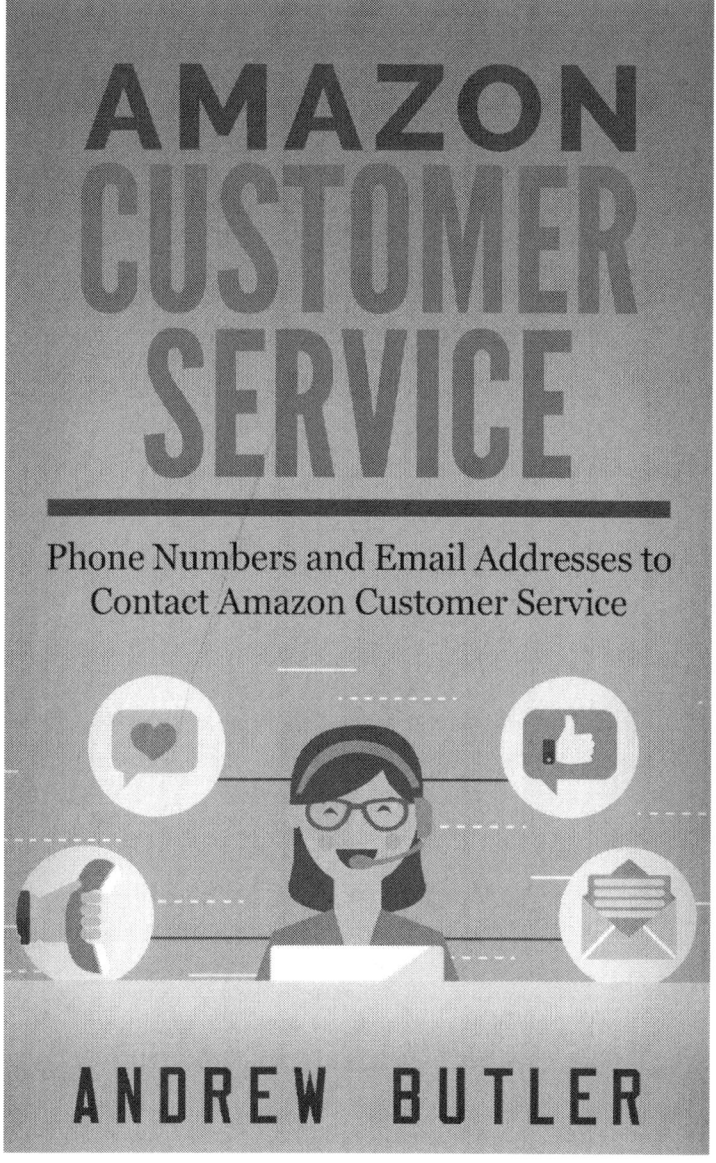

Java: 2017 Ultimate Beginners Guide to Learn Java
Programming

Fire Stick: The Ultimate Guide for Beginners to Using your Fire Stick to the fullest

Printed in Great Britain
by Amazon